SPEARFISHING

BY S.L. HAMILTON

Visit us at
www.abdopublishing.com

Published by Abdo Publishing Company, a division of ABDO, PO Box 398166, Minneapolis, Minnesota 55439. Copyright ©2015 by Abdo Consulting Group, Inc. International copyrights reserved in all countries. No part of this book may be reproduced in any form without written permission from the publisher. A&D Xtreme™ is a trademark and logo of Abdo Publishing Company.

Printed in the United States of America, North Mankato, Minnesota.
102014
012015

PRINTED ON RECYCLED PAPER

Editor: John Hamilton
Graphic Design: Sue Hamilton
Cover Design: Sue Hamilton
Cover Photo: AP
Interior Photos: Aimrite-pgs 4-5, 8-9, 23 (inset) & 30-31; AP-pgs 28 & 29; Cressi USA-pgs 12-13, 14-15, 16-17 & 30; Corbis-pgs 18-19 & 22-23; JBL-pg 32; Justin Garnett-pg 9 (atlatl insets); iStock-pgs 1, 2-3, 7, 20-21 & 26-27; MAKO Spearguns with freediver Brian Pucella-pgs 10, 11 & 24-25.

Websites
To learn more about Fishing, visit booklinks.abdopublishing.com. These links are routinely monitored and updated to provide the most current information available.

Library of Congress Control Number: 2014944879

Cataloging-in-Publication Data

Hamilton, S.L.
 Spearfishing / S.L. Hamilton.
   p. cm. -- (Xtreme fishing)
ISBN 978-1-62403-684-2 (lib. bdg.)
Includes index.
1. Spear fishing--Juvenile literature.   I. Title.
799.1/4--dc23

2014944879

Contents

Spearfishing

Spearfishing is a hunter-versus-prey challenge. This type of fishing has been practiced for thousands of years. Many of today's hunters use lightweight but powerful spearguns. Others fish close to shore using traditional pole spears.

Divers enter an underwater world and come face-to-face with their prey. Spearfishing is an exciting, heart-racing hunt that pits one human against one fish.

XTREME FACT –
People who spearfish are sometimes called spearos, or spearfishers.

History

Spearfishing can be traced back to when humans first started using tools. Ancient Egyptians documented their spearfishing techniques in their paintings and sculptures. More than 5,000 years ago, they spearfished from shore, as well as from small boats.

An Egyptian is shown spearfishing in a wall painting from the tomb of Usheret in Thebes, Egypt, from around 1430 BC.

Ancient Greeks fished with spears and tridents around 150 BC. Sculptures of Poseidon, the Greek god of the sea, show him holding a trident, or three-pronged spear. Pacific Islanders and Native Americans have spearfished for thousands of years. As long as people have used tools, spearfishing has been a way to catch prey.

A statue of Poseidon with his trident.

Pole Spears

The most basic way to spearfish is to use a pole spear. It is a sharpened stick used in shallow water. Adding barbed points improves the chances of striking prey and keeping it on the spear.

XTREME FACT - *A tool called an atlatl allows spearos to throw a spear harder and farther than they normally could. It is a combination fishing spear and slingshot.*

Hawaiian Slings

A Hawaiian sling can be compared to an underwater version of a bow and arrow. This simple-but-effective spearfishing tool became popular in the 1950s and continues to be used today.

XTREME FACT– Everything underwater looks about one-third **BIGGER** than it actually is. Spearos keep this in mind as they search for prey. They don't want to go after a target that's too small.

A Hawaiian sling consists of rubber tubing attached to a wooden shooter. The launched spear travels farther than a pole spear. Hawaiian slings can be used in areas where triggered guns are not allowed.

Pneumatic Spearguns

Pneumatic (new-mat-ick) spearguns use compressed air to shoot the spear out of the gun. These powerful guns shoot thicker spears a great distance with good accuracy. They are often used to hunt large fish. A pneumatic speargun is usually armed with a spear by using a hand-held loader. To safely discharge a pneumatic speargun, it must be shot underwater.

Loader   **Spear Shaft**   **Spear Tip**

Cressi's Saetta pneumatic speargun uses a spear that fits inside a sealed internal barrel. A shaft loader tool is used to push the spear into the barrel. The white handle makes the speargun easier to find if it's dropped on the sea floor.

Smaller pneumatic spearguns are easier to load and carry. Larger ones may require special loading tools, but can be used on very large fish. On the negative side, pneumatic spearguns make a loud noise when they are shot. This warning noise may spook the prey and allow it to escape.

XTREME FACT– Spearos sometimes have their catch taken by larger predator fish, such as sharks.

Band-Powered Spearguns

Band-powered, or "banded," spearguns use high-tension rubber bands to shoot the spear. This is a very popular type of speargun. Spears are shot accurately and nearly noiselessly.

Band-powered spearguns are often easier to aim. An open-muzzle banded speargun shows the entire length of the spear's shaft. This helps the diver line up the shot. However, the spears are usually thinner than ones used in pneumatic spearguns. They may bend or break off when they strike large fish.

XTREME FACT– To make a more powerful weapon against larger fish, additional bands are added to the speargun.

Shafts, Tips & Lines

Modern spear shafts and tips are made of hardened stainless steel. This metal resists rusting and bending. The spear may be barbed or have a "flopper." When the spear shoots through the fish, the flopper flops open (or "engages") and rests on the outside of the fish's body. Barbs and floppers prevent the spear from pulling back through the hole when the spearfisher reels in the shooting line.

The shooting line is attached to the spear's shaft at one end and to either the speargun, a gun-mounted reel, or a float line. Lines are often made of monofilament, Kevlar, or stainless steel cable.

XTREME FACT – Spear tips come in many designs, depending on the type of fish being sought. Pencil-nose and tri-cut tip points are common. Pencil-nose points are used on thinner-skinned fish, such as yellowtails and mackerels. Tri-cut points are used on thick-skinned or scaled fish, such as groupers or snappers.

Shoreline Spearfishing

Many spearfishers enter the water from beaches and shorelines. They may fish in waters up to 82 feet (25 meters) deep. Spearos search for their prey in rocks, kelp, and coral. However, beaches and shorelines draw many recreational users. To protect people's safety, most countries do not allow spearfishing next to the shore. Spearfishers must check local regulations to find out where they can safely fish.

Scuba Spearfishing

Some spearfishers use scuba gear to stay underwater for longer periods of time. This allows them to hunt for larger fish at deeper depths. Scuba spearfishers may dive down searching for such fish as grouper, flounder, and snappers.

To spearfish with scuba gear, divers must be scuba certified. One of the problems with scuba spearfishing is the visible bubbles that emit from the diver's exhaled breath. This is a warning to fish.

XTREME FACT – Scuba spearos are sometimes nicknamed "bubbleheads."

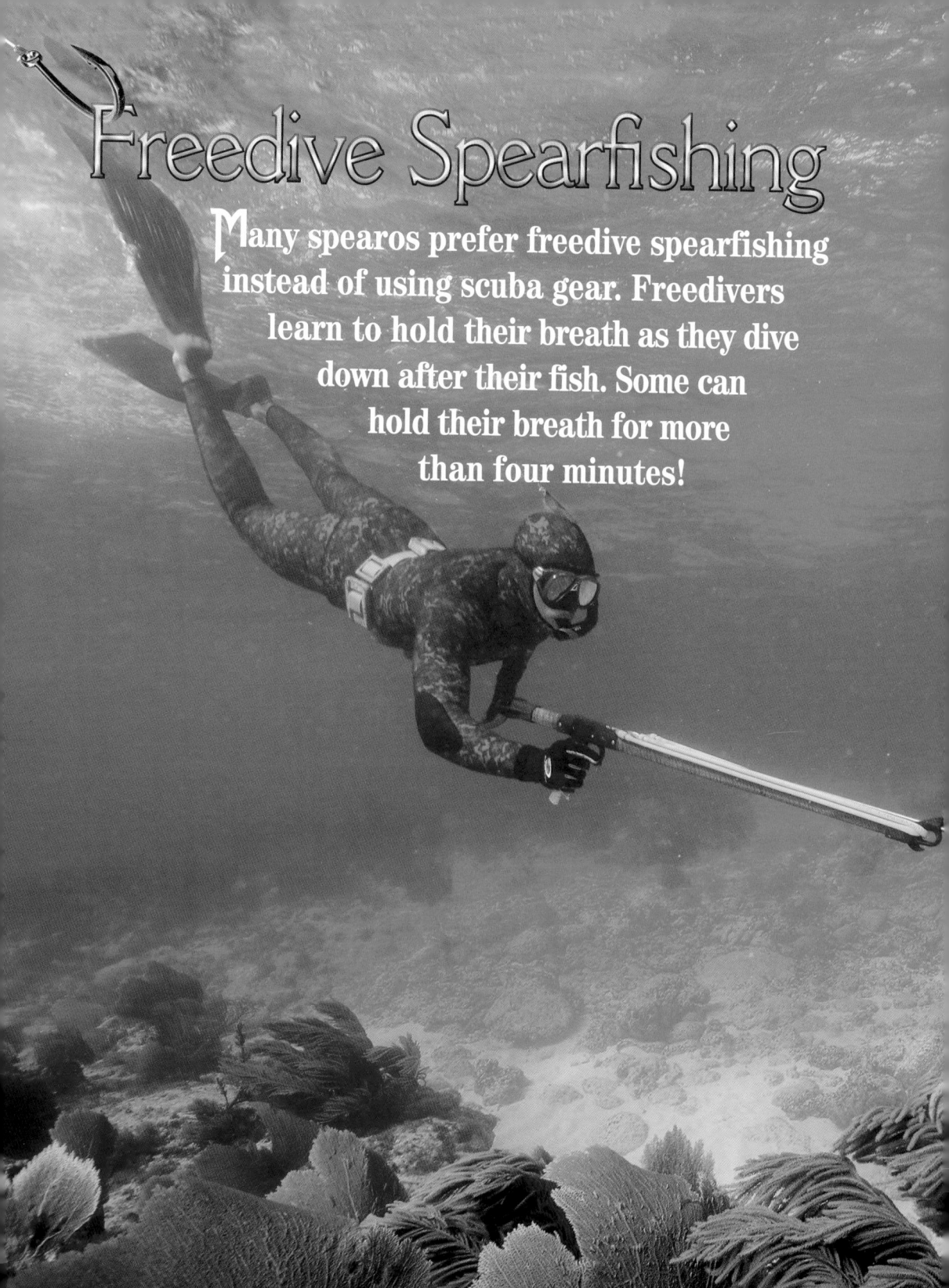

Freedive Spearfishing

Many spearos prefer freedive spearfishing instead of using scuba gear. Freedivers learn to hold their breath as they dive down after their fish. Some can hold their breath for more than four minutes!

It is very challenging to swim down, spear a fish, and return to the surface with the fish in tow. This type of spearfishing takes training. It is important to have a buddy at the surface to help if something goes wrong.

XTREME FACT – All spearfishing world records are based on fish caught while freediving. The International Underwater Spearfishing Association defines spearfishing as "the capturing of a wild game fish through the use of a muscle-powered speargun, while freediving."

Ocean Spearfishing

Ocean fish such as grouper, tuna, dorado, and marlin are big catches for spearfishers. One of the advantages of spearfishing is that the hunter can select a specific prey. Fish that are protected or endangered are left alone. Most spearos follow the motto: "Don't know. Don't shoot." They also follow the rule to take only what they are going to eat.

Freediver Brian Pucella with a grouper.

XTREME QUOTE– "... You are immersed in the undersea world as you come head to head with the very fish you are trying to catch."
–Steve Andrews, spearfisherman

Freshwater Spearfishing

Spearfishing in freshwater lakes and rivers is difficult. Inland waters are often muddy. Rains, flooding, and algae blooms make it difficult to see fish. Additionally, swimmers, waterskiers, boaters, and other fishermen are usually on lakes and rivers, and it is illegal to spearfish near people.

Spearfishers are restricted by which fish they can take. In most of the United States, only "rough fish" are hunted. These are larger fish that are not commonly eaten, such as carp, gar, bullheads, and suckers. A few states allow spearfishing of game fish, such as sunfish, crappies, striped bass, catfish, and walleyes. Spearos must check the rules for the state in which they plan to hunt.

XTREME FACT – In the spirit of "use what you take," spearos who hunt fish that won't be eaten often donate them to zoos, or use them as fertilizer or bait.

Dangers

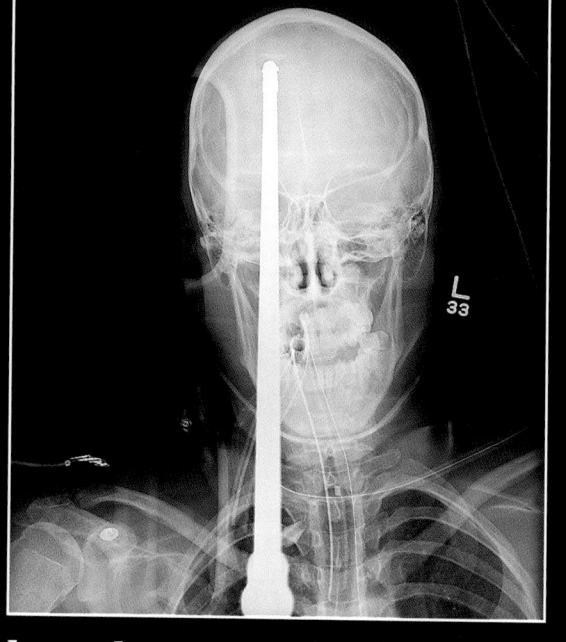

Spearfishing is a sport with a unique list of dangers. The accidental discharge of a speargun can cause serious injuries or death. Freedivers who overestimate how long they can hold their breath risk blackouts and drowning. Shoreline spearfishers risk getting hit by waves and smashed against the rocks or seafloor. Shark attacks are possible when big predators go after a diver's bleeding prey, or the diver. As with any sport, training and safety are important.

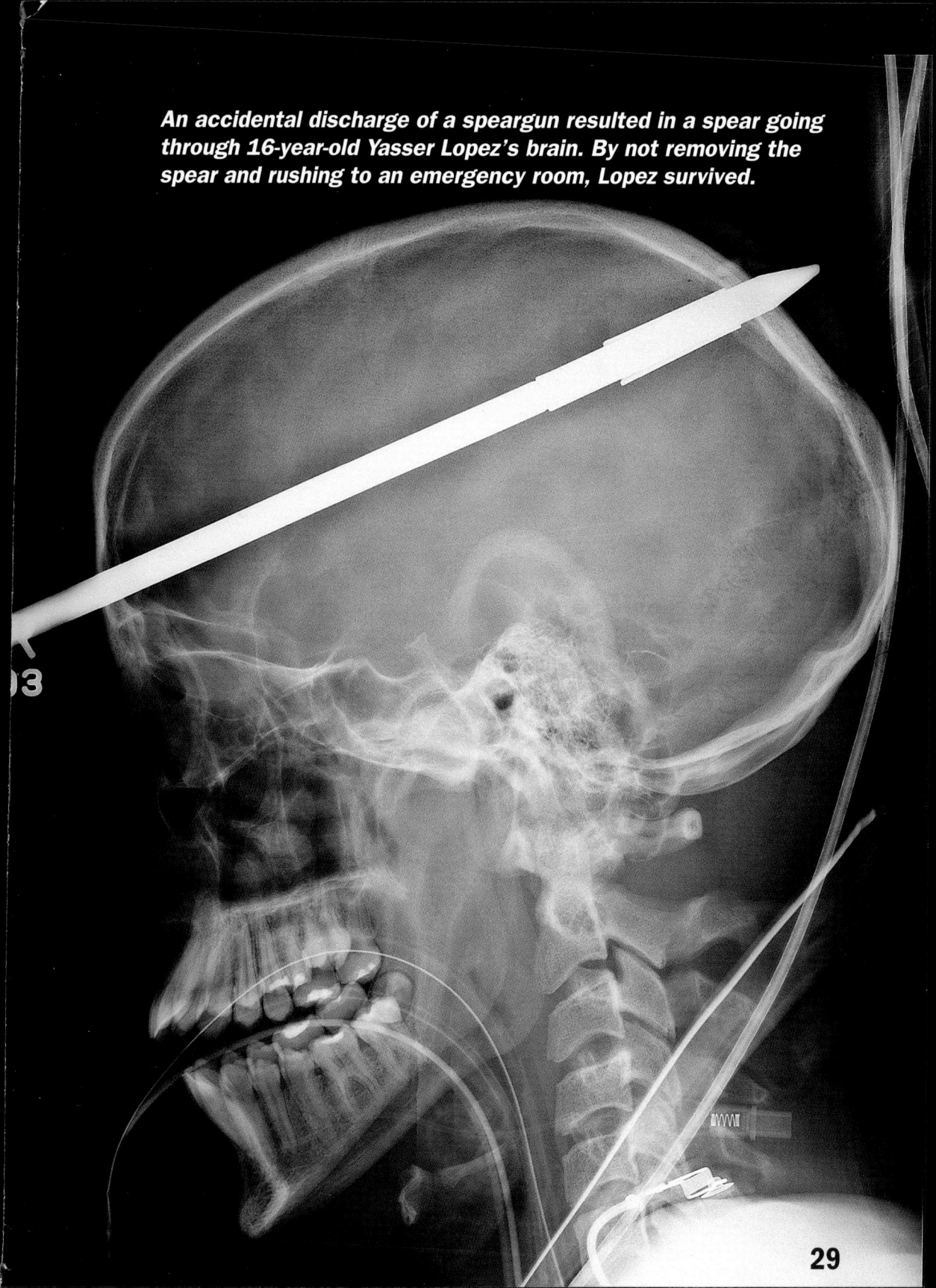

An accidental discharge of a speargun resulted in a spear going through 16-year-old Yasser Lopez's brain. By not removing the spear and rushing to an emergency room, Lopez survived.

Glossary

ALGAE BLOOM

When an algae (small plants) population suddenly grows much larger. A bloom will cause the surrounding surface water to turn a green or brown color.

BARB

A sharp projection, such as found on a fishhook or a spear tip, that catches on the fish and prevents it from being pulled out when the fish is reeled in.

BLACKOUT

When a person loses consciousness. Also known as fainting. Blackouts may be caused by a lack of oxygen to the brain.

FLOAT LINE

A strong line, sometimes made of stretchy bungee material, that connects a speargun to a buoy floating on the surface. It is used to help hold a big fish and to prevent it from dragging a diver underwater. The float line is attached to the speargun. Yellow and white float lines are easy to see. Red, blue, and black are nearly invisible underwater for stealth.

FREEDIVING

To hold one's breath and dive underwater. Freedivers may hold their breath underwater for several minutes.

International Underwater Spearfishing Association

A group organized in 1950 to maintain spearfishing world records and to promote lawful and safe spearfishing practices.

Kevlar

A light and very strong man-made fiber. It is sometimes used to make shooting lines in spearfishing.

Monofilament

A clear, flexible fishing line made of a single strand of artificial substances, such as nylon. Monofilaments come in many strengths.

Pneumatic

A tool operated by pressurized air or gas.

Scuba

Scuba stands for "self-contained underwater breathing apparatus." It is a device that allows divers to breathe underwater for a certain period of time.

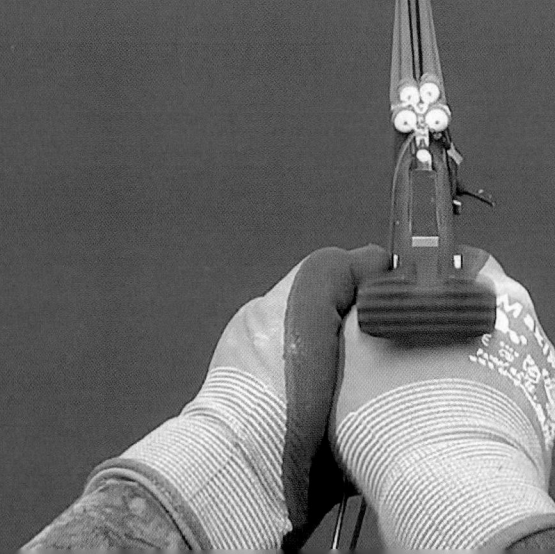

Shooting Line

A strong fishing line that attaches a spear to a speargun. The shooting line is pulled or reeled in to retrieve the catch.

Stainless Steel

A type of metal that is strong and resists rusting. Spears are often made of stainless steel.

Index